A Heart Divided

A shocking true story of abuse,
gender confusion... and *hope*

CARMEL
HICKLING

real stories. real hope.

wildsidepublishing.com

Published by Carmel Hickling in association with Wild Side Publishing
www.wildsidepublishing.com

Email: overcomerkazi@gmail.com

Cover concept Carmel Hickling. Graphic design and text layout by Janet Curle, WSP. Cover copy by Ray Curle, WSP.
www.wildsidepublishing.com

Cataloguing in Publication Data:
Title: A Heart Divided

ISBN: 978-0-473-56764-4 (paperback)

Subjects: Christian Memoir, Gender Confusion, Inspiration, Spirituality, Body Soul Spirit, Christian, Non-Fiction, New Zealand, Mission, Christian Living, Homosexuality, Lesbian, Identity, Sexuality.

First New Zealand printing, April 2021
International listing, Ingram Spark, April 2021

contents

dedication

To all who have ever
fought and struggled
to find out who they are,
and to Sharnee,
a beautiful soul,
who I miss dearly.

endorsement

If God has put this in your hands to read, you will not escape His message of love through Carmel's powerful testimony.

The most powerful message is that her circumstance has not changed on the outside, i.e. disease, but her changes within and without—in spite of this world's strife—speak to the power of relationship with the Father heart of God to hope, and faith and life to overcome. A message very important as Christians can judge people by the fruit of their life, yet God weighs the heart.

In this current environment of fear, panic and anxiety, suicide, and the spirit of death and hell clashing with God's message of hope, this book is a tool that points towards God's power over death.

This book is not just for Christians, and Christians with a religious and judgmental spirit will be convicted. It is for people searching for their identity, purpose, love, hope and God too—and needs to be published *yesterday*!

—Vania Lamont, Baylys Beach

foreword

I want to commend Carmel's story to you.

It is raw, it is challenging, it is distressing at times, but it is also full of hope, it is powerful—and it is straight from the heart.

Carmel is very brave to lay her life experience so bare for all to see—and for that, she deserves our utmost respect.

As Carmel states in the Dedication, this book is for all who have ever fought and struggled to find out who they are.

That's me. That's probably you as well.

As you read Carmel's testimony, may you—like Carmel—also know more of God's peace, freedom, courage, wisdom, truth and grace.

> *"If you continue in My word, then you are truly My disciples; and you will know the truth, and the truth will set you free."*
>
> **John 8:31-32 (NASB)**

—Bob McCoskrie, National Director, Family First NZ
www.familyfirst.nz

prologue

This is my story of love and of hate, of lies and of truth, of worthlessness and of pain, of despair and of hope, and of the hunt for victory.

I cannot help but be a tad envious, of my friend when she tells stories of her childhood and of her loving, doting parents. It is almost like a fairy-tale, or a yarn of fantasy and vivid imagination. It is the pure, unadulterated truth… however, that is her truth, and her story.

It makes me ask the questions… WHY and WHY NOT?

I believe that writing this book will help to heal my heart, and who knows, maybe you will find some healing in it too.

introduction

Born in 1969 in Porirua, Wellington, New Zealand, I am the seventh child of eight. I have five sisters and two brothers.

My Dad was an alcoholic and Mum was a strict and very religious Catholic. Mum taught us good morals and ethics. We all knew right from wrong.

I grew up in a time where there was no internet or mobile phones. Televisions were black and white. Cars were for the rich. We were dirt poor.

There was no emphasis on mental health or suicide prevention. You did not share your thoughts or issues. You handled them by yourself.

Abuse comes in many forms and from many people. Psychological. Verbal. Physical. Sexual. Control. Financial. I guess we all dealt with Dad's abuse differently. We all found our own way to retreat and try to escape.

To this day, I still have a close bond with some of my siblings, but not all of them. I cannot share their stories. I can only share mine.

Carmel

a heart divided

I have not always believed in God. Sure, I went to church, but I didn't always believe. I do now. Definitely.

100% Believer. 65% Faith. 50% Trust, but working on it.

I know God is real without any doubt. I believe in Him, but at times, I find it so difficult to believe what He says.

It has not, nor has it ever been easy. Not by any means at all. I think I fight Him more than I pray to Him, and yell at Him, more than I praise Him. He loves me anyway. Nothing I do, or have done, will ever change that. It would have been great to know that truth when I was a child, but I guess God had other plans for me.

Not one of us knows why God does things the way He does. I hate the journey that God has me on right now. I am absolutely terrified. I have no control of anything. I have so many unanswered questions and prayers. I am afraid of the vulnerability it has brought me. I am afraid to be unprotected.

I thought hard about adding this next part to my story, and chose to do so because my downward spiral played a huge part of my journey in overcoming the darkness, in the hunt for victory.

I have been sick for around four years now with no answers, and it is at its worst now. I lost my voice for eight months. I have had over 40kg of unintentional weight loss. Yes, I have had to change what I eat, quite simply because swallowing is extremely difficult. I only ate yoghurt for 6 months. I find it difficult to breath.

Two days out of seven, I might have a bit of energy. Half the time, I have no voice. My ears and eyelids now too, are always getting infected. My immune system is non-existent. My head feels like there is a clamp tightening on it, it has the similarity of a severe concussion, and I get electric shocks up and down my throat, across my cheeks and in my head. The pain is an unbelievable burning, with the added sensation, that I have been hit in the face with a sledgehammer.

... my downward spiral played a huge part of my journey in overcoming the darkness, in the hunt for victory.

Firstly, it was once every so often. Now, it is every day.

Yes, God can do anything, but whether or not He chooses to, is another story. Sometimes, it is His plan and will, for you to go through things.

Most Christians are all about God healing, so I went for prayer.

I got prayer. No healing.

More prayer. No healing.

LOTS of prayer. Still nothing. I lost a little bit of hope.

I was told that my faithlessness was the reason that I did not receive any healing. After 12 months, I was told that I must be in sin to not be healed.

I do not know if hurt or pride rises in those who pray for others, if their prayers go unanswered, or if they see it as a blemish or stain to their faith, but after the first 6 months, I was told that my faithlessness was the reason that I did not receive any healing. After 12 months, I was told that I must be in sin to not be healed.

A little bit more hope left.

People did not know what to say to me, so they did not say anything. Doing that just made it worse.

Nobody wants to talk to someone who is in

deep depression.

I withdrew more. I went to church to do my job as sound technician and left straight after.

I felt like these people thought I was bothering them and they did not want to pray for me. So I did not ask again.

I guess people are still people. Intact with all their traits. Good and bad. Even me.

Nobody wants to talk to someone who is in deep depression. I withdrew more.

After two years, I had slight hope that I would still receive healing. After three years, I had little encounters with God here and there, but ultimately hope had long gone. Anger had taken place of hope and unbelief had taken the place of prayer. I hated God. Where was His love? Where were his promises? I was sure He was still punishing me.

I could not understand it. Why me? Had my life not been enough of a mistake? I obviously must still deserve it.

Then, I gave up entirely. My want had changed from being healed, to wanting to die. I was so weak that I could not even walk or eat. The strongest painkillers did nothing for the pain. I could not understand it, because I knew God is real. Where was He? What had I done wrong to deserve this? Was it because of my past?

One particularly hard night, my lungs and ribs too, felt like they were going to explode. I had found my limit, and I begged God repeatedly, to let me die.

There was a deafening silence. I heard a song, faintly at first, then it grew louder, and then it played repeatedly. It was, "You're Gonna Be OK," by Jenn Johnson.

Then Jesus appeared in my room, and although she was singing, they were His words. He took my hand and said, "All I ask of you is that you fight to stand in the hope of who I AM."

Then Jesus appeared in my room, and although she was singing, they were His words. He took my hand and said, "All I ask of you is that you fight to stand in the hope of who I AM."

He sat down and held me in His arms and I felt like the most loved person in the universe. I knew that He would leave millions, to rescue one lost soul, because in that moment, I was that lost soul.

None of my devices were playing any music. This was all Him.

The song continued all night and when I awoke in the morning, it was still playing.

I sat up and tried to find the song on my laptop, and when I found it, I cried uncontrollably and He was there again.

I tried to stop crying and He said ever so gently, “Don’t stop, you need to grieve for what you have lost, and for what you will lose.”

He answered questions that I had asked, and told me things that I needed to know. Every night, I still begged Him to let me die.

I cried for hours and hours and He held my hand the entire time.

The next day, He made me a playlist on Spotify and He named it HOPE.

He answered questions that I had asked, and told me things that I needed to know.

Every night, I still begged Him to let me die.

The next day, He sent my sister, who said she was not prepared to stand around and do nothing, while I waited to die, since I had given up the will to live.

When she left, He showed me heaps of people, and when I asked who they were, He answered, “They are the ones who will be lost forever, if you are not around."

My prayer did not change. I did not want to live. It was too hard. Too much pain. I was too far gone. It was too far back.

The next day He sent me visitors.

My prayer did not change. "Please just let me die."

Every day, more people were added to the first lot of people, He had shown me. My prayer still did not change.

The next day, He showed me thousands upon thousands of people, and when I said that I did not know hardly any of them, He said, "The first lot of people, upon encountering you, would have a chain reaction to everyone else, and none would perish."

I looked closer at them all, and right at the front were my great nephew and great niece, both under 5 years old.

I changed my prayer, and I asked Him to give me the courage to find the will to live, and to eat.

I changed my prayer, and I asked Him to give me the courage to find the will to live, and to eat.

The next day, He sent my sister and the mother of those two beautiful children. They brought a huge hamper, filled with things that I could and might be able to eat, and more importantly, swallow. He sent people with soup, pureed, so I could sip it slowly. It took ages, and every mouthful hurt as I swallowed. My body had already gone into starvation mode. The tremors were terrible, but I got to a place where I could eat a few solids, like toast.

That night, I collapsed and fractured my wrist. Those thoughts came back... 'Where is He? Does He not care anymore?'

I lost all of my muscle.

Then He left.

That night, I collapsed and fractured my wrist.

Those thoughts came back...*'Where is He? Does He not care anymore?'*

I was not impressed that I had to spend the night in hospital, but they replaced the much-needed fluids that my body lacked.

When I look back now, I think that maybe He was fast tracking those fluids because of the pain I had swallowing.

The wrist healed ok.

It took a long time to walk properly again, and it still hurts to walk.

Who knew butt muscles hurt so much!

After that amazing week with Jesus, when He left, I was annihilated. I got so angry again, because I was so sure I was going get better, but I got worse.

Everything got worse. EVERYTHING.

Then one day, He said that He wanted me to want Him, more than I wanted to have healing.

I already had nothing. No life. I barely existed and He wanted me to choose Him! Had He not taken enough from me?

Over the next few months, I slowly lost all reasoning and hope, and headed into my downward spiral.

I found myself contemplating driving my car, through the crash barrier into the river below. However, the river was too low and I most probably would not have drowned.

So then I sat on the edge of a HUGE cliff, willing it to give way, but I decided that with my bad luck, I probably would end up a quadriplegic, and not be able to move, let alone escape my life.

I found myself contemplating driving my car, through the crash barrier into the river below.

Driving down the highway, in the distance I saw my way out. My escape was in the form of a huge black truck. It looked like it had twenty-eight wheels, and in that small amount of time, I gave it the name, "Black Death." I increased my speed, calculating where the best place to hit the truck would be, to cause the most damage and surely end my life. I could not do it; because I knew that the reality of being in an accident with a fatality would destroy the driver forever. I wanted to end my life, not wreck his.

Driving down the highway, in the distance I saw my way out. My escape was in the form of a huge black truck. It looked like it had twenty-eight wheels... I gave it the name, "Black Death."

So yet again, this is where I found myself, once again looking for an escape.

I screamed at God, "Why do I always run away? Why do I always feel the need to escape? Why can't I see and accept you as a Father? Why do you hate me so much? Why is it always so hard? Why? Why? Why?"

He is taking me back to deal with my past. To sift through and find the pure truth that lay hidden behind all the lies.

lies

I have always been afraid of living. I always thought that I was never good enough. Not for my Mum and certainly not for Dad.

My Dad told me when I was eight that if I wanted his love, I should become his little boy and forget being a girl, because they were useless and worthless, and so I did. He even changed my name to Harry, and I was his boy in all things, except in the physical sense.

My aunty even thought that Harry and Carmel were identical twins, not just one person.

Dad was verbally abusive and used to launch horrendous attacks on all of us. Sadly, I used to help him pick on my eldest sister, who was overweight. I was Dad's little mate. He loved me. I was wanted. I can remember setting the lounge carpet on fire accidently, and he did not blame me at all. I could do no wrong. He shared his flagons of beer with me, and we smoked cigars and cigarettes in the basement. Life was great.

I really believed I was a boy, and then puberty hit.

When my body started to change with all the girl parts, my Dad lost interest, and told me that I was just a weak, useless, worthless girl. Good for nothing but having babies and doing women's work.

With those words, I developed intense bitterness and self-loathing. I tried to win his love back but he did not care. He was not interested in me. I used to pick fights with other kids, who I knew would absolutely pulverise me, because that was all I deserved. If my Dad did not want me, I was not worth anything.

I really believed I was a boy, and then puberty hit. When my body started to change with all the girl parts, my Dad lost interest, and told me that I was just a weak, useless, worthless girl.

I remember when Mum and Dad talked of splitting up, and we kids were asked who we wanted to live with. I yearned to get Dad's acceptance and love back, so I asked him if I could live with him.

I found out in that conversation that love hurt

much worse than hate ever could.

Soon I hated Dad with a passion. I hated all males. I hated my brothers too because they had an air of entitlement about them. I hated females as much as I hated males.

I seemed to be both, and so I hated myself more.

I lived somewhere in the middle of where love and hate collided.

useless

I never wanted to be a girl because I believed that they were weak, useless, worthless, and good for absolutely nothing but having babies and doing women's work. In all essence, I was nothing but a man's slave.

Years later, when my sister got married, I could not stop crying, because I thought her husband was taking her away to be his slave. I did not think I would ever see her again.

Mum was a Catholic at the time, so we had to go to church, which I hated. I hated the priests who made the women do all the work, and they got all the kudos. I hated that I had to call them father. Just another man trying to make me a slave to his will. I hated my own father. I did not need a replacement father. I grew to hate God too. I believed that He hated me, because He called homosexuality an abomination.

I cannot remember exactly when I knew that I was a homosexual.

However, I remember many churchy people accusing me of sacrilege and calling me a monster.

I believed that I was worth less than a slave because they had a purpose and I had none; a million Hail Mary's could not save a homosexual.

I remember wondering if Mum knew she was a slave. I knew that I would never get married to a man. I would never be a slave.

I was unsure of my feelings toward Mum. She was always so busy; she worked hard at two jobs, one on nightshift. She did washing for other people, as well as raising eight kids, keeping the household together, and putting up with my abusive and alcoholic father. She was not weak, and did not appear to be useless or worthless, and her God hated me.

I believed that I was worth less than a slave because they had a purpose and I had none; a million Hail Mary's could not save a homosexual.

I used to think that it would hurt too much to love her. I know she did her best under the circumstances. I mean, really, she was a single parent considering dad was drunk all the time.

Mum had to be both parents.

She always provided enough. Enough clothes. Enough food. We always had a bus ticket for school (unless we lost it). Mum went without so we did not have to. Despite being dirt poor, she always made sure we had fun. She would go the extra mile for us. I know that she loved us.

As much as I yearned for acceptance and love, love had become my greatest enemy.

LOVE… Love had torn my heart to pieces.

Love let in vulnerability. Love brought hurt. Pain. Rejection.

As much as I yearned for acceptance and love, love had become my greatest enemy.

It is funny the things you remember. It was such a different time back then. As much as things were crap, I had many great times. Sometimes I could stop trying to figure out who I was, and have fun. We played back yard softball, and all the neighbours played. All the neighbourhood kids hung out together.

We had to walk everywhere. Cars were only for the rich. One of my favourite memories is when we would go to watch my sister play soccer.

We had to walk about seven or eight kilometres to the game, and we would look for money on the road. Someone on each side. If there was time, we would go up the little side streets too. Whatever money we found, we used to buy baked potatoes from Homestead Chicken, after the game. They were 4 cents each. It was our treat.

I can remember finding a 50-cent piece and I was over the moon. That bought twelve potatoes alone.

That day, I was a hero. That day I mattered. That day I had worth.

nothing

Mum told me I was confused. "You are a girl, act like it!"

Even though I had girl parts, I still thought of myself as a boy.

I did not want to be a girl because I believed they were useless and worthless, and it hurt too much to think of myself being nothing.

Nothing!

That word has to be one of the worst words in the entire history of words, in any language. To label someone as useless or worthless, gives rise to the thought that one would at least have been considered for some task and failed, but considered nonetheless.

NOTHING means exactly that—Nothing. A void. A waste.

I had come to understand that I was useless and worthless because I had failed God. I started to think that I was nothing because I was both a male and a female, but I was also neither a male or a female. I had no purpose.

No purpose. No point. No worth. Nothing.

I started to think that I was nothing because I was both a male and a female, but I was also neither a male or a female.

I saw that men had an air of entitlement. They walked around as if they were kings. Women were their slaves.

I could never understand why women were okay to be those slaves. They just did the work. Some even appeared to be happy in their work.

I remember hearing a song and the lyrics went:

Put another log on the fire.
Cook me up some bacon and some beans.
And go out to the car and change the tyre.
Wash my socks and sew my old blue jeans.
Come on, baby, you can fill my pipe,
And then go fetch my slippers.
And boil me up another pot of tea.
Then put another log on the fire, babe,
And come and tell me why you're leaving me.

(song by Tompall Glaser)

Men never had to do anything.

Women cooked. Men ate all the food.

Women cleaned. Men made the mess.

Women had two jobs. Men drank away the money.

Women ran the household. Men sat around.

Women did the laundry. Men just dirtied it.

Women tended to the children. Men complained about them.

Women did everything. Yet, men were head of the home.

Men had the final say. Men were dictators.

Man of the House. A Man's Legacy.

Slave. A Woman's Legacy.

Not me. No way. Never.

I could never understand why all my friends dreamed of meeting their future husbands. They could not wait to be someone's wife. A mother. A family.

I knew I could never have that.

I knew I would never marry.

I knew I would never have children of my own.

I was not entitled to anything. I was nothing.

My way of thinking was so messed up that when a person

I could never understand why all my friends dreamed of meeting their future husbands.

spoke to me, I would hear something completely different.

They said, "Carmel, can you clean the toilet?"

I heard, "I'm too good for a menial task like that, you do it Carmel, you are nothing."

Or,

"I'm not available to do that sorry."

I heard… "I'm more important than you, I come first. Your plans are nothing compared to mine. You do it."

People would ask everyone out for lunch, forgetting to ask me, and I saw it as me not being good enough. Nothing.

People would ask everyone out for lunch, forgetting to ask me, and I saw it as me not being good enough. Nothing.

I got so used to being overlooked that it confused me if I got a compliment. I would make an excuse as to why I did not really deserve any credit and how they were wrong in their assumptions of giving me praise.

Sometimes my hurt would arise as anger, and I would "lose it" at people. Ultimately, I saw them and their lifestyle as completely out of my reach. We were worlds apart.

Them. Loved. Worthy. Wanted.

Me. Nothing.

Not worthy. Not good enough. Nothing.

My whole life I thought like that. Even now I still sometimes do.

I guess it is because I have been so entrenched in the belief that I truly am nothing, and I have no worth.

"God made you a girl for a reason," Mum would yell. I thought that if God created me, and hated me for being a homosexual, then what was the point of listening to Him or doing what he wanted, when I was his creation. I was His fault.

I never saw myself as a man. I was only ever a boy. It was as if I was stuck in time.

I was not a slave, yet I held no entitlements. I had no legacy.

I was a monster. A mis-creation. A mistake. Nothing good.

No worth. No value. I was nothing.

I tried to be and act like a girl, but I did not know how. Honestly, I still do not know... and I am now 50 years old. It is not as if I can just put on a dress, grow my hair and POOF, instant femininity.

She was right though. I was confused. I had a boyfriend to hide the fact that I had a girlfriend.

escape

I learned early how to deceive and I became quite the expert in the art of manipulation.

I found that if I was really "good" and polite to the nuns at the Catholic convent, then I got to go away on lots of camps / trips to the South Island. I could escape my life for a while.

I could be whoever I wanted to be when I was away.

I could be someone who everybody wanted to be friends with.

On my 13th birthday, I had my first thoughts of suicide. My friends from school came to my house. I saw the goodness and normality in their lives and I saw how far away it was from my grasp.

One of my sisters is an epileptic, and that night, for the briefest of moments, I had the opportunity and thought to swallow all of her pills, and then POOF, the thought was gone.

After my birthday, I started drinking more. I made friends with kids whose parents were more than generous with alcohol. We used to shoplift and steal from houses to pay for alcohol.

I managed to drink so much one night, that I got alcohol poisoning and nearly died. I was most disappointed that I lived.

At my school, a boy had hung himself with his shoelaces, and so I tried with my shoelaces too. And wouldn't you know it, they broke. Every time.

At my school, a boy had hung himself with his shoelaces, and so I tried with my shoelaces too.

And wouldn't you know it, they broke. Every time.

I did however, manage to drown myself, quite by accident. I can remember the absolute peace of just letting go, giving into it, my sought after escape… and then, a kind person resuscitated me.

I started to gang up on Dad with my older sisters. I remember one night when he came home drunk and had a go at us, we beat him up good. My sister smashed a plate over his head and I stabbed him with a fork. My brothers had a go at him too. It felt so good to fight back. It felt better to win. It felt amazing to have control.

I had found a new friend. Its name was Control.

My lies and pretence had allowed me glimpses of a type of freedom. They were nothing compared to Control. Control gave me a kind of power, and power allowed me to do things my nothingness would not let me do. When I could not handle something, Control took over and put up all the walls necessary to contain the problem. I thought I had found the answer to my freedom.

Walls were built. Many walls.

Dad became much more wary of us after that. We were growing up, we were getting stronger and faster, and he was getting scared.

Things changed at home, Dad was given an ultimatum from Mum; his family or his alcohol. He went away for a while to dry out at some place, and then when he came back, he never drank alcohol again. He was still very abusive though. His words still could cut through my walls, like a knife through butter.

Control gave me a kind of power, and power allowed me to do things my nothingness would not let me do.

As much as I hated Dad, I still yearned for affection from him.

More walls went up.

There is a saying that goes…

Sticks and stones may break my bones,
But names will never hurt me.

What a total lie!

You lavish a person with love and see them overflow in the confidence and self-assuredness of who they are.

You lavish a person with verbal and psychological abuse and you watch them wither in fear and insecurity because of who they are.

You lavish a person with verbal and psychological abuse and you watch them wither in fear and insecurity because of who they are.

Many, many walls. And still more walls.

I remember watching a documentary about Brenda Spencer, a young girl who shot kids at a school in America. When asked why, her reply was, "I don't like Mondays." Years later in prison, she was found to have the words, "Unforgiven and Alone," etched into her skin via a knife.

I knew the feeling of being unforgiven and alone all too well.

Then I moved out.

I thought I was free from judgment, but I could never escape my self-loathing.

I thought I was free from the pain of being unloved, but my intense hatred made it worse.

I became the best at whatever I put my hand to, but I was never satisfied.

Being drunk and drugged up helped for a while, until my lack seeped in, taking hold and blocking the escape that I had found.

Over the years, I drank and did as many drugs as I could, but I still felt completely empty inside.

I became the life of the party, but by morning, I was once again nothing.

I could always hear Dad's words:

useless — weak — worthless

Then my words:

abomination — mistake —nothing

Being drunk and drugged up helped for a while, until my lack seeped in, taking hold and blocking the escape that I had found.

I still hated people. They were so two-faced. It disgusted me when I attended funerals of suicide victims when people would say, "Oh, if only he would have said something," or, "He just never got over that really… couldn't put it behind him."

When? When did you give him time? When did his time line of grief override your time limit? When were you so open that he felt safe to come to you? When did you truly care?

Yes, people sucked!

hunted

Then one night, as fate would have it… or God for that matter, I found myself as the driver in a head-on collision. Car versus cow, then a tree, for good measure. I died on impact. I remember seeing the cow's face come at me through the windscreen, and then nothing… at least for a while.

At some point, I could smell the sickly aroma of fresh blood and then I was above my body. Later, I would tell of things that were impossible for me to know, since I had died on impact.

I was floating, but I had no body, and I could see the carnage that the cow and tree had done to my car. The steering wheel had bent backwards with the force of the impact and the body (me) in the car was a mess, to say the least.

The engine had been pushed towards the inside of the car, and was pretty much sitting on my lap. My legs were under the engine somewhere. Half of my face was mush, glass was stuck everywhere in it, and it was not a pretty sight.

Then, the floating me, turned and I was back in pitch-black darkness again. It was dark for ages and then randomly I could see things that looked like red laser lights. The lights became clearer and I saw that they were in pairs. Then, some yellow with brown lights appeared. The lights were eyes piercing the darkness.

I remember feeling dread. Terror. FEAR.

There were whispers, "*She's mine... get away...*" I had an eerie sense, that I was being hunted. I did not have a body, but I was being pulled in all directions; I could feel it as if I had a body. There was growling and what sounded like meat being ripped apart.

I remember feeling dread. Terror. FEAR. There were whispers, *"She's mine... get away... "* I had an eerie sense, that I was being hunted.

Then from out of nowhere, a huge wall-like object was in front of me. It was alive. It moved. It was the colour of skin, and it seemed to be made of skin and flesh. It had faces of people and they were screaming in agony. There was an awful smell.

Suddenly, although I had no body, I felt a horrendous pain where my shoulder would have been.

Darkness. Then back to the wall. Pain.

This happened three or four times.

Meanwhile, back at the car, help had arrived. They had sorted out my passengers first, because I had been declared as dead. Then, after a while, they were getting my body out of the car.

At the wall, I felt a searing pain in my legs (but no body — very odd).

At the car, apparently, I let out a scream and then nothing. They all freaked out. Checked my pulse again and yep, I was still dead.

Again, I felt a searing pain in my lower back and at the car, I yelled out ***STOP!***

Quick as lightning, they stopped what they were doing. I remember saying, "My legs are stuck in the motor. My shoulder is broken and so is my back, so stop pulling. *You're killing me!*"

I had no idea that I had been dead for quite some time. Then I went back to

"My legs are stuck in the motor. My shoulder is broken and so is my back, so stop pulling. You're killing me!" I had no idea that I had been dead for quite some time.

the darkness. Back to the wall.

Back to being hunted.

Psychologically however, I was not good at all. I had nightmares about what I had seen, what had hunted me, and what was still trying to get me.

Suddenly, I was back in the car, in excruciating pain. No more wall. With my instructions, the rescuers were able to pull me out of the wreck, intact except for half a tooth.

Physically, everything healed. I have decent scars and even screws for my war stories. It took me a year to learn to walk without a limp, and about the same for my eyebrow to grow back, but I was most happy that I had not lost any limbs.

Psychologically however, I was not good at all. I had nightmares about what I had seen, what had hunted me, and what was still trying to get me. I feared the darkness for many years.

I was scared of driving at night. I was deathly afraid of what was hidden in the dark.

I dabbled in the occult and witchcraft in a bid to find out what had happened, or rather where, I had gone.

I found with the witchcraft, that if anyone

wronged me, I could go to an alternate reality and hurt that person. Then, in real time, they would be hurt the same. I had complete power and control. This went on for a few years.

I survived for a few more years, using witchcraft as an escape, and then it all fell apart again. The circumstances are not important, but I was completely broken.

As fate (or God) would have it, I had to move back into town with Mum and Dad.

I was now around 26-years old, and most of my family had moved up from Porirua, Wellington, to the middle of the North Island of New Zealand.

I found with the witchcraft, that if anyone wronged me, I could go to an alternate reality and hurt that person. Then, in real time, they would be hurt the same.

I sat on my bed and yearned for an escape. As I put all those pills in my mouth and the water up to my lips, I heard a whisper. "But what if it's not lies." Pills came out. I looked for the whispering culprit. Nothing.

Pills back in, water up to lips. Another whisper, "What if it's not all lies? What if God is real?"

All throughout my life, I had heard titbits of God being love. I craved acceptance, even though I was afraid of love. I always thought God hated me. I had always thought that He was punishing me. The God that I knew of did not like me at all.

Could He love me? Would He love me?

Pills out. Eyes to the ceiling. Words from my mouth. "God, if you are real, then show me, but, I want to know without a doubt. I'll give you 24-hours, then it is pills back in."

I went to sleep. I woke up and nothing was different. Same room, same rubbish, same crap life. The God of love was a lie.

light

I needed to go inside the main house to use the toilet, and when I opened the sleep-out door to go outside... ***BOOM!***

God hit me with His reality. I was speechless. I instantly knew things about people. I saw the talents that He had gifted to them. Words cannot describe what I saw. The colours of everything were the deepest, brightest, most vibrant, most WOW!

It was as if God had coded the clouds in the sky for me to decipher. I did not I know it but the best was yet to come.

In the book of Genesis in the Bible, it says, "In the beginning God created the heavens and the earth. The earth was formless and empty, and darkness covered the deep waters. And the Spirit of God was hovering over the surface of the waters." (NIV)

That is where God took me. In that moment, I saw the Spirit of God hovering over the waters. It is still the most spectacular thing I have ever seen.

There are NO words to describe Him.

The amazingness of the Northern and Southern Lights do not even come close. Not even a bit. That is how I came to know God is real. Without a doubt.

There are NO words to describe Him. The amazingness of the Northern and Southern Lights do not even come close. Not even a bit.

100% Real.

I never felt like I belonged anywhere, until I found God. The real God, not the one people had threatened me with, and lied about.

I thought that everything would always be okay. I expected to feel amazing every day.

I thought that along with salvation (ticket to Heaven), I would get a better life. I thought that all my problems and issues would leave. I would be free. I would never ever again search or yearn for a permanent escape from my life.

With good comes evil. There is always an enemy.

An invisible enemy. It is spiritual warfare.

I am pulverised by the enemy. Every day. Every moment.

Just because I had God in my life, did not mean things would come easy. It is not easy to be a

Christian. I never realised that I needed healing for my heart.

I never knew the way I saw things was wrong.

People would say, "You need to let go of things."

I did not know what. I did not know how.

I was still not sure if God truly loved me. I felt different, but I did not recognise the feeling. I could not give a title to the sensation I felt, when God was around.

I knew God was real, but I still had all the same thoughts.

I thought I had to prove myself to people. When they did not listen to what I had to say, I knew that I was still nothing.

I was still NOTHING. No worth. No purpose. No legacy.

turmoil

Then Dad got Alzheimer's disease and Dementia. I had to help Mum look after him.

This man who I blamed for ruining my life, was now in my care.

I still hated him. I confused him even more.

I mocked him and disrespected him every chance I got.

I used him. I tricked him into giving me cigarettes and cash.

Elder abuse had nothing on how I treated him.

I hated him more. I had fun at his expense, whenever I could.

He lost all memory of what he had done. He had got away with it.

I had visions of me smothering him with a pillow. Every day.

Some days upon waking up, I had to go and check that I had not actually done it.

Yes, I called myself a Christian.

Yes, my hatred was still very much a part of me.

Yes, I still hurt.

Yes, I wanted revenge.

Dad eventually went into a rest home.

He had "practices of dying" quite a lot. When Dad was in hospital one night, Mum made me go and visit him.

He looked like a scared little boy. I was pleased. Inside I was hoping that those things, that had hunted me in the darkness, would rip him to shreds. I wanted to see him suffer.

God was convicting me to forgive him. Right there. Right then. I was so conflicted and tormented. I was a heart divided.

God was convicting me to forgive him. Right there. Right then.

I was so conflicted and tormented. I was a heart divided.

I was once again, in the middle of where love and hate collided.

In the end, I came to a place within myself, where I could somewhat forgive him.

I expected to feel amazing and free, but I just felt… numb.

He whimpered like a little dog, and he reached for my hand.

And he said…"Harry."

I slapped away his hand. He was faking it. He was not sick.

He had to pay. He was NOT forgiven. I left.

That was the last time I saw him alive.

I was at home playing a game, when my sister rang and told me Dad had died, and we were all going to meet up at the rest home.

I continued doing what I was doing. I just did not care.

Too much hurt. Too much pain. Too much hate.

I have always been great with words and poetry.

God gave me the words, and I wrote Dad a poem.

At his funeral, it was not until I started reading it out to Dad that I saw who he was. The real him. The sad, unloved, hurting and lonely little boy. I wanted to go back in time and just hug him, and take all his hurt and pain away.

In that moment, freedom came as I forgave him. I did not hate him anymore.

In that moment, freedom came as I forgave him. I did not hate him anymore.

Later, I asked God why Dad was like the way

he was. He showed me that when Dad was a boy, his mother was sick. She was a staunch Christian, so Dad prayed to God, asking Him to heal his mother, and she died. Dad never forgave God, and turned his back on love.

I had masterfully learned to reject others first, and I saw how Dad had done it all his life. In a sense, I had mirrored my father.

I had masterfully learned to reject others first, and I saw how Dad had done it all his life.

In a sense, I had mirrored my father. I was a sad, lonely little boy, so afraid of the hurt and pain that came with love.

A few years passed and at some time, Mum had a serious heart attack, and since I was the only single one with no kids, we decided I would go and live in the sleep-out and help her around the house.

I have done this, happily, for many years. I got a job just around the corner too, so it worked for both of us, and we both had our own space.

Then one of my brothers came to live there.

Suddenly, it was as if I had become a slave to a man.

I still did the gardening, mowed the lawns, pruned the trees, stacked the wood, and cleaned out the chicken coop. I did it all.

Yet, he had the title of Man of the House. It was his legacy.

He had walked in and taken the title, simply because he was born male.

He never did anything to earn it.

He had stolen my place of safety. It was now his domain.

He was a dictator. He started making rules. His narcissism made me invisible. I became second to him. I was once again nothing.

On a Christmas Eve, my mother told me that she wanted me to help her make two dips for the dessert and drinks evening. She planned on having it at her house the following night.

He had walked in and taken the title, simply because he was born male. He never did anything to earn it.

I went to my sister's house for Christmas dinner, and upon returning to Mum's afterwards to make them, Mum was upset because I didn't help her make all the desserts and other food.

I told her that I thought it was only two dips and that my brother had been there all day anyway.

Her reply, "Ohhh, but he wanted to have a

sleep, and it's not really what men do; it's women's work."

That made me ANGRY!

Man of the House. A Man's Legacy.

Slave. A Woman's Legacy.

I am not a slave.

I hated that men did nothing to receive their title.

I hated the saying, 'Boys will be boys.'

As I look back, after her father died, Mum had grown up slaving for her brothers and stepfathers. 'Man of the House' and 'Head of the Home,' were all terms she grew up hearing. Her life had been put on hold. Men came first. In her eyes they still did. They always would.

Women were pathetic. Women were worthless slaves. I was not a slave. That would never be my legacy.

Women were pathetic. Women were worthless slaves.

I was not a slave. That would never be my legacy.

I still hated men. I hated them more now.

Man of the House. Head of the Home. Dictators.

Some men were different though. They did not treat women as slaves. They treated women like queens, like royalty. To these men, women were their equal. These men intrigued me.

There were not many of these men around, but they amazed me when I came across one.

These men provided for their families. They did work around the house. They shared the load. They showed love. They were not dictators. They loved their children. They cared. They earned their Legacy. They did not just take it.

Some of them even wanted to talk to me. They truly seemed interested in what I had to say.

I wanted to know what made these men different. What made them act this way?

My sister's husband was one of these men, and another sister's partner was, too.

truth

I thought that I truly deserved every bad thing that happened to me. People would tell me that I had been forgiven but I never felt it. All I ever felt was guilt. Guilt of being a monster and a mistake. Guilt of being born. All I ever saw was the distance in comparison. The worth of others. The nothingness of who I was.

Today, I realise that I was running away. I was running from my own judgment. I was running from love. I was running from the truth. I have been running my whole life.

I was never free, not once.

The walls did not protect me; they shut me in.

I had NO power.

Control was not my friend. It was my brutal enemy.

Control was Dad's protection; it protected his hurt.

God never hated me. He detests the sin, the act of homosexuality, because it takes away the purity of who He created people to be.

And LOVE… love didn't hurt as much as hate.

That was the BIGGEST lie of all.

God never hated me. He detests the sin, the act of homosexuality, because it takes away the purity of who He created people to be.

Love is still very hard for me to deal with. With love comes vulnerability. Vulnerability leaves me open and unprotected.

Open to hurt and pain.

Love is a choice. A choice to trust.

Mum had been away for a week, and when she came home, I hugged her tightly and told her I loved her. She said, "You must have missed me." Under my breath I replied, "I have missed you my whole life."

In that moment, I realised that I have.

Too afraid of rejection. Too afraid to try. Always afraid to love.

I am still dealing with the value of women, the idea of slavery and my dislike toward most men, and I am still dealing with who I am.

I have always wanted to go to one of those women empowering women conferences, like Sistas, but I always thought I never quite fitted the criteria to go.

My friends are bona fide women. I am not. I am a little boy.

I knew a woman once, and we grew to be quite good friends. Nothing more, just a platonic friendship. One day someone asked her if I was her girlfriend. They had thought that she was gay, simply because she and I were close. She will no longer talk to me. We are no longer friends.

It breaks me a little bit more every time that happens.

I am afraid to go on road trips with other women especially if we have to share a motel. I am afraid of that rejection.

I expect it to happen. I expect the rejection. So I reject others first.

Even at my church, there seems to be no place for me to fit.

Even at my church, there seems to be no place for me to fit.

About thirteen years ago, God said to me, "I have set you apart for MY purpose." I am not sure if not fitting in, is what He meant.

Jesus told me one day that He wanted me to know what it is to be the daughter of a King. I have found it to be an extremely hard and painful journey so far.

Since I have only ever seen myself as a boy, I only ever bought men's clothing. I now own three pairs of women's shorts, and three or four nice tops, and I even bought some black dressy 'girl boots', as I call them.

Baby steps.

I am now the opposite of who I was. I have to rely on God.

His Strength. His Provision. His Way.

In my years of despair, I made myself as repulsive as I could. I did this by overeating during this time. I now weighed in at a whopping 130kg.

I have dropped over 40kg through this sickness. Everyone says I look amazing and I am starting to think I do too. God has such a sense of humour, in how He does things. I could not have done it alone. He made sure the right people were always around me.

Before I got sick, I used to be able to mow seven lawns a day. Now I am only able to mow one a week, if that.

I guess before, I relied on myself.

My Strength. My Provision. My Way.

I am now the opposite of who I was. I have to rely on God.

His Strength. His Provision. His Way.

I am trying to live a bit more positively and kick negativity to the curb. I fail at this most days (NEARLY ALWAYS). I still try.

I am still competitive and do not like to lose, especially to an enemy that is deceitful, and who does not fight fairly.

All my life, I did things so people would hate me, because I could deal with hate. Reject first before they reject me.

Now, I do things for what I am pretty sure are the right reasons. Not to find self-worth. Not for praise. I do things for others because I want to, not because I have to.

I am not a slave.

I am learning to accept, but still find it extremely difficult to receive criticism, constructive or not. Sometimes, I liken the words to being shot at with a machine gun; the words, being the bullets.

Worthless. Useless. Not good enough. No chance. Unloved. Alone. Unforgiven. Unwanted. Nothing.

I am still competitive and do not like to lose, especially to an enemy that is deceitful, and who does not fight fairly.

I know I am none of those words, yet sometimes, they still seep in. Hurt and pain, leave many scars and open wounds.

Suicide is such a misunderstood action. Victims of suicide are declared as selfish and 'just thinking about themselves', amongst other things. I understand suicide perfectly. It is not so much that death is the answer, or that death is the ultimate goal. If you look back on a Suicide victim's life, you will see that they will have tried many different ways and things, to find an escape. Escape from their issues, escape from judgment, escape from themselves, escape from their thoughts, and escape from lies that have been drilled into them as truths.

Suicide is such a misunderstood action. Victims of suicide are declared as selfish and 'just thinking about themselves', amongst other things.

I tried so many different things to escape. I am not talking about heavy drugs; they came when everything else fell apart.

I am talking about building invisible walls to protect myself.

Not letting anyone in because of my fear of the pain that love brought. Everything I tried, worked for a while but then slowly, my "safe place" began to disintegrate, every time. All these things were just a temporary respite.

Suicide brings forth the thought of a permanent escape.

Despite the fact that I have a relationship with God, my life is still a hard journey. Every day the darkness tries to take me back. To lure me back into the pits of despair.

I still wonder if I will ever get well health wise. I guess it does not really matter so much to me now. It is funny how things change. Physically, I am still in as much pain as ever, but healing is not my number one priority any more.

I have learned that faith does not mean trusting God to STOP the storms of life, but trusting God to STRENGTHEN me as I WALK THROUGH the storms.

I have recently learned that faith does not mean trusting God to STOP the storms of life, but trusting God to STRENGTHEN me as I WALK THROUGH the storms. I have stopped asking God for healing. I now ask for strength to get through the moments.

The daily moments. The hard moments. The painful moments. The unbearable moments.

I still find it hard to trust people. I still think they are going to use and abuse me. I do not understand why they like me, or how they can love me. I would rather be alone, than to talk to people.

God is working on that, too.

Baby steps.

I do not fully know who I am yet, but I know who and what I am not.

I am NOT a monster. I am NOT a mis-creation, and I am definitely NOT a mistake.

I am NOT a homosexual. I am NOT interested in anyone, and I am quite happy with that decision.

Most churches or believers do not discuss or talk about homosexuality, except to say that it is wrong. Maybe it is not enough to tell people what they are doing wrong. They need to know why.

I am Carmel. I am Me. I do not need a title to be worthy.

Most churches or believers do not discuss or talk about homosexuality, except to say that it is wrong.

Maybe it is not enough to tell people what they are doing wrong. They need to know why. Plant the seed. Then we need to let God do His work.

I have found that God is the ONLY one who can heal.

He knows us intimately. He knows the intricacies of our delicate being. Physically. Emotionally. Spiritually.

It needs to be His process. His timing. His love.

He knows us intimately. He knows the intricacies of our delicate being. Physically. Emotionally. Spiritually. It needs to be His process. His timing. His love.

I guess God has set me in an ideal position to see both sides.

I understand completely the incessant need and yearning for acceptance and love.

Like any relationship, you find someone who is your place of safety. You find love. Acceptance. Freedom from judgment.

I understand completely the emotional connection found with the same sex. I also understand why it goes beyond that.

You have acceptance of love. You want more. The purity of love then is soiled with the act of sex.

Thus, sex and love become synonymous with each other.

The next steps would be Marriage. Children. Family.

I hear of women who leave their husbands, and vice-versa, and then enter into a relationship with the same sex.

I understand this completely as well. Everyone just wants to be accepted and loved. If they do not get that acceptance with the opposite sex, some will try with the same sex. These days, people look for love with anyone, anywhere and wherever they can find it. The line between *love* and *lust* becomes blurred.

love vs hate

God is love, and so we must be that love to others. He may give us the position of teachers, but the curriculum is His, and His alone.

If we add our opinions to it, as Christians, we can come across as self-righteous and condemning. We can put others off God. Maybe forever.

I remember in my early days of being a new Christian, the Civil Union Bill was being debated in Parliament. Many people were going to the "Enough Is Enough" march against it. Some of the people in my church were taking a bus down to Wellington to be part of it.

I was not sure of how I felt about it. I was torn.

Once again, I was a heart divided.

I stayed home. I watched it on TV, and I was disgusted.

It was a hate-fest. It was manic.

It had become a brawl.

It was supposed to be truth versus lies, but it was opinion against opinion. Man versus man.

Woman versus woman.

Hate versus hate.

There is no them and us. There is only us. Us humans. Us sinners.

There are those who know the truth of Jesus, and those who do not.

I saw many self-righteous people pointing and yelling at others saying, "*You are living a lie,*" and "*God will judge you harshly.*"

I really felt for the people. The people who did not know Jesus. Some people have felt like nothing their whole lives, and the Christians had just made them feel worse.

I really felt for the people. The people who did not know Jesus.

Some people have felt like nothing their whole lives, and the Christians had just made them feel worse.

Christians always talk about the love of God and of how God is so forgiving. Where was that?

I do not know about you, but that would have put me off God forever, if I did not already know He was real.

I know as Christians, we need to stand up and speak the truth, but if we do not speak in love, it becomes our self-righteous opinion.

It becomes about rules. Even if they are righteous rules. We become slaves to keeping those rules.

I am not a slave.

When I was new to the church thing, a few godly women stated that I was confused, and that my whole life was a lie.

I see now that they were trying to help. Trying the only way they knew how.

It did not help me at all.

I already felt that I did not matter. Their words just confirmed the fact that I was nothing. Now, according to them, even my entire life was nothing. I may as well be dead.

I know that God looks at, and deals with the heart. He works from inside to out.

Perhaps as godly people, we should be doing the same.

When I was new to the church thing, a few godly women stated that I was confused, and that my whole life was a lie.

Everyone has a story. A journey. A testimony.

Every person has had a mess turn into a message.

Good and bad. Right and wrong.

If God is the ultimate judge, then who are we to judge others?

I once saw a poster of a face with duct tape over its mouth.

The caption said, *If you do not have anything nice to say then…*

Maybe we should all carry a roll of duct tape, just in case.

I was once asked to speak to the youth group about the topic of love. I said that I could not because I did not know what love was. I only knew what love was not.

I was once asked to speak to the youth group about the topic of love. I said that I could not because I did not know what love was. I only knew what love was not.

1 Corinthians 13:1-3 says,

> *"If I speak in the tongues of men and angels, but do not have love, I am only a resounding gong or a clanging cymbal. If I have the gift of prophecy and can fathom all mysteries and all knowledge, and if I have a faith that can move mountains, but do not have love, I am nothing. If I give all I possess to the poor and give over my body to the flames, but have not love, I gain nothing."*

Many people in the world today, know what love is not.

I guess, knowing what love is not, gives me an unseen connection with these ones.

The word 'nurture' comes to mind. We need to nurture the lost, the hurting, the messy, the escapees, the hard, the runners, the dejected, the used and the abused, the used up, the forgotten, the never loved, the invisible and the nothings.

We need to nurture them on the journey from outcasts to overcomers.

We need to nurture the lost, the hurting, the messy, the escapees, the hard, the runners, the dejected, the used and the abused, the used up, the forgotten, the never loved, the invisible and the nothings.

When we are born, we are born with legs. It takes a while for us to learn how to use our legs. With every step taken, our legs become stronger. Our legs hold us up. If injured, our legs falter, and we cannot stand so well.

People teach us to walk, and how to continue to walk when injured.

I guess that is how I see my relationship with Jesus.

When I found out He

was real, I had to learn more about Him. How to walk. How to be strengthened, and amidst injury, how to still be able to stand.

People can talk about love. People can share about love. People can even show their love for you. People cannot touch your heart and provide the healing it needs like Jesus does.

I had people who taught me to walk.

They never taught me how to stand, when injured.

Only Jesus can do that. Only His Love can do that.

People can talk about love. People can share about love. People can even show their love for you. People cannot touch your heart and provide the healing it needs like Jesus does.

People cannot teach us to STAND in the HOPE of WHO HE IS.

Only Jesus can do that. Only Jesus laid down His life for mine.

Only Jesus can give the true definition of love.

Only Jesus. Only Him.

In the Bible, Romans 8:35-37 says,

> *Who shall separate us from the love of Christ? Shall trouble or hardship or persecution or famine or nakedness or danger or sword? As it is written, "For your sake we face death all day long; we are considered as sheep to be slaughtered."* No, *in all these things we are more than conquerors through him who loved us.*

More than a conqueror. I like the sound of that.

We cannot do it alone. We cannot do it just with people.

We are only more than conquerors through Him who loved us.

We need Him. We all need Jesus.

overcomer

Thoughts of suicide still cross my mind most days. I shake them off. I know this is the unseen enemy trying to pull me back into the darkness.

I am retreating into God. I realised today that I no longer want to escape and withdraw from my life. I want to escape and retreat into Jesus.

When I gave up entirely a few months ago, He said to me, "All I ask of you is that you fight to stand in the Hope of Who I AM."

I guess that is what I am trying to do. It is very hard.

It is me fighting against every lie I have ever believed, and choosing to stand firm in my faith and belief of who HE IS and what He has done.

It is me, holding my ground, despite all the circumstances and craziness that surround my every moment.

It is me, standing firm in the HOPE of what HE DID for me.

It is me believing the Bible to be the pure Word of God.

It is me laying my life down and offering it to Him, to do His will and further His Kingdom.

It is me becoming less of me, and more of Him.

He is asking me to trust Him. Trust what He has for me.

Trust that He has my back. Trust that He is all I need.

Trust His love.

He asked me to take off my security vest, and to lay down all the weapons I use to protect myself. To lay down everything I use to keep myself safe from hurt, pain, and rejection.

He asked me to take off my security vest, and to lay down all the weapons I use to protect myself. To lay down everything I use to keep myself safe from hurt, pain, and rejection.

He asked if I would allow Him to be my safety.

He asked if I would be open to love and the vulnerability it brings.

He asked if I would allow Him to be in charge.

He did not take. He did not dictate. He did not demand.

He asked.

I choose YES.

It is a daily decision.

Every day I have to make a conscious choice to let Him be in charge.

I have only ever seen myself as that little boy, stuck in time.

I see now, that I was afraid to be anyone other than him.

In that moment in time, he was loved. He had worth. He could do no wrong.

Through writing this book, I am no longer the little boy. I am not sure who I am yet, but I am definitely not him anymore.

I have been talking and wondering all my life about my legacy.

I have no legacy. I have a Destiny. It is Jesus. Only HIM.

Together, God and I are sifting through the lies and the truths of my past, and this book is part of that journey.

I am fifty-years old now, and yet He takes me back to the point in my life just before Dad, served me the lie.

Through writing this book, I am no longer the little boy. I am not sure who I am yet, but I am definitely not him anymore.

I am standing with Jesus watching as this scenario unfolds. I am eight-years old and I am just sitting there, eagerly waiting for some time with my dad. I just want to pick up the young me and run far away from him, and the lies that would ensue. I wanted to save her from the life that I have had, never knowing the truth, and always believing the lies.

When I look back, I can now see God's fingerprint from where He went before me, making a way through for me throughout every aspect of my life.

As much as it breaks my heart, to leave the young me there, I know that God is healing this once heavy heart of mine, through these moments of the past.

When I look back, I can now see God's fingerprint from where He went before me, making a way through for me throughout every aspect of my life.

The shoelaces breaking. The pills.

The kind person who resuscitated me. The whispers.

The fractured wrist. The car accident. Even this terrible sickness.

I was deceived and lied to, and those thoughts of being nothing still hammer me, but with God's help, I am and will, conquer them.

Baby steps.

So yeah, none of us knows why God does things, the way He does.

Maybe, if I did not get so sick, I would not have found my limit, and I would not have hit rock bottom so hard.

Maybe I had to go through all of this, so I could show others the way to the truth.

We are not useless. We are not worthless. We are NOT nothing.

We are not slaves. We have a pre-ordained destiny.

We are MORE THAN CONQUERORS.

I have travelled back in time. He is showing me everything, and is righting the wrongs, caused by the truths smothered by lies.

It is still a most difficult journey.

restoration

Many people have the expectation, because I am over fifty now, that I should know better, or they say that I should act my age.

In saying that, I have only just stopped being the scared little boy.

I guess that LIFE as a journey, builds our character, and as God slowly moulds and shapes who we are; He reveals our identity to us. God does it in His own time. Our age makes no difference to His process nor to His schedule.

After forty-two years of believing lies, and searching for my identity, there is a lot of healing needing to be done. I know I am getting that now.

I am slowly changing, and with each step, my mind and heart are slowly healing.

Baby steps.

In the Bible, Joel 2:25a says, "*I will repay you for the years the locusts have eaten.*"

This means restoration. If it is written in the Bible, which is God's Word, then it is a promise from God.

I know that with every step in the healing process, so too, will God bring about restoration in my life.

I always knew what love was not. Jesus is showing me, and teaching me what love IS.

For years, I hated my dad, now I do not. Restoration.

For years, I wanted to escape my life, now I do not. Restoration.

For years, I believed love was my enemy, but it is not. Restoration.

I always knew what love was not. Jesus is showing me, and teaching me what love IS.

I am slowly learning that it is ok to be vulnerable. The vulnerability that once terrified me is ok. It is ok because I have Him.

It is ok to care for others. It is ok to choose to love. It is ok to be hurt because of love. It is ok because I have Him.

I have started accepting compliments from people. I have started to accept that my church family care and love me. I can do this because I have Him.

I have started to accept that I am worth something, and that I am not nothing. I can believe this because I have Him.

I have started to show care and love for others,

although there are still some people that I have not yet learned how to love. For now, I just have to accept them for who they are, not for what they do.

I am sure God will teach me one day.

Baby steps.

I guess now, I can see the pain in other people. The pain of their past, the pain of their hurts, and their vulnerability. I can see how and what they have used to escape.

I want to help them find the path to victory.

To be an Overcomer. To find the truth. To be free.

God told me the definition of an Overcomer. It is someone who refuses to give in to failure. Someone who keeps trying. Even if they retreat for a time, they come back and try. Someone who, against all odds, still stands even if standing means they are a complete mess. Someone who holds on, even to a mere thread of His garment. Someone just like me.

I guess now, I can see the pain in other people. The pain of their past, the pain of their hurts, and their vulnerability. I can see how and what they have used to escape.

I have discovered that only God can take everything that is messy and broken in my life, and do something amazing with it.

I have discovered that only God can take everything that is messy and broken in my life, and do something amazing with it.

Only God can. Not man. Not me. Only God.

Only with LOVE. Only with His love.

1 Corinthians 13:13 says, "*And now these three remain; hope, faith and love, and the greatest of these is love.*"

I can see why. Without love, there is no purpose. Every person yearns for love, acceptance and worth, amongst a vast array of other things.

freedom

I have found that God is many things, but what truly stands out to me is that God is Freedom.

Freedom to choose. Freedom from judgment. Freedom from guilt. Freedom from turmoil. Freedom to just be me.

Without Freedom, we can become religious. It becomes about rules. It becomes a dictatorship. We become slaves.

I am not a slave.

If you want to know if God is real, without a doubt... you know what to do. Be prepared to have your mind blown.

Be prepared for a life unlike any other.

Yes, there will be highs. Amazing highs. Unexplainable joys.

There will also be lows. Unbelievable rock bottom lows.

But God has you, safely in His hands.

You are loved. Incredibly. Always. Unconditionally. Forever.

You are a like a seed. Every day you need nurturing to grow. The elements will try to take you out. Some may for a time, cause you to wither and droop, but you will continue to grow. One day, you will bloom into the most perfect and beautiful creation.

But Jesus did not die only to only make me SAFE; He died to make me DANGEROUS too!

Trust the process. It is all about the journey.

The journey to forever.

The journey to FREEDOM.

The journey to safety.

But Jesus did not die only to only make me SAFE; He died to make me DANGEROUS too!

I have often wondered why the enemy has tried so many, many times to take me out. All the darkness that he heaped on me in the past, was intended to destroy me, but with God's direction and instruction, it will become a dangerous weapon.

It was the enemy's plan to push me over the edge into permanent darkness, and although it took years and years, I went THROUGH the darkness towards the light.

Towards freedom. Towards victory. To Jesus.

I can see the threat that this book will have to

the enemy and his deceitful schemes, plans and ploys.

To all who read this, I pray that any lies in your life will no longer hide the truth, and that my story brings forth healing from the onslaught and barrage of hurts and pain that have assaulted you in your life's journey.

It is my heartfelt wish that you will see that there is a way through the suffering and the darkness.

His name is Jesus. You might know Him as HOPE.

For all of my entire life, I have never felt safe. I do now.

Jesus makes me feel safe. His safety gives me the courage to try, to try to do anything despite any risk of rejection, pain and hurt.

I know that I will be ok. I know because I have Him.

I trust in the Hope of who HE IS.

There is a saying that

I pray that any lies in your life will no longer hide the truth, and that my story brings forth healing from the onslaught and barrage of hurts and pain that have assaulted you in your life's journey.

goes,

'Be the kind of woman that when your feet hit the floor each morning, the devil trembles in fear saying, "*Oh no, she's up!*"'

God told me recently, that is who I am.

a heart complete

For years, I blamed God for allowing the situations and circumstances that I found myself in. I yelled and wrestled with Him nearly every day.

Now when I look back at the whole scenario, I see that God was making me deal with all the issues at once. He was fast tracking me.

I absolutely hated the way it came about, but I learned to embrace the journey.

It would not be called LIFE if it was not hard.

He used the situations to my advantage, and I guess to His.

Just like it says in the Bible, I really am similar to a lump of clay.

He moulds and shapes me every day, twisting and kneading, getting the impurities out so He can bring forth His perfect creation.

Who He sees me to be—not who and what others see.

During the Covid-19 lockdown, God taught me about moderation. I forced myself to do some gardening every day. I did not do hard-core, full noise, over the top kind of work, as that kind of energy is non-existent now. He taught me that chipping away little by little was ok. He showed me that He was doing that with me, from the inside out.

I still do not understand why some people receive instant healing and others do not.

I do get why God has not healed me from this awful disease. I guess if I was completely well, I could do most things in my own strength and steam.

I do get why God has not healed me from this awful disease. I guess if I was completely well, I could do most things in my own strength and steam.

I need Him to help me breathe a lot of the time, so I HAVE TO invite Him into the situation to help me through the pain, and to get through the day.

Because I have personally invited Him, I tend to feel more at peace. I do not feel like I am being FORCED to be in the process, to slog it out alone, or that this is a punishment.

We are in it together. Him and I.

Everything that I have been through has been for my good.

To correct. To discipline. To heal my heart. To find freedom.

To share. To help others.

Sure, I still get frustrated at times, but I have learned to ask Him for strength, courage and wisdom to get through the hard yards.

Instead of fighting God, I am learning how to let Him fight for me.

I learned what and who HOPE is, and what it is to have joy in the dark times. I can have joy in the hard trials because Jesus is with me through it all to the end. All things are possible with Him.

I have learned about expectancy and intimacy in God.

I am in relationship with Him. It is not about rules or religion; it is about Him and I.

I learned what an *overcomer* was in His sight, and I became one.

I have learned the hard lesson that value and acceptance must come from Him and from myself—not from other people.

Instead of fighting God, I am learning how to let Him fight for me.

I have a knowing within myself that whatever may happen, I will be safe.

He is my anchor.

He is my refuge.

My steadfast place of safety.

It defies human logic that although I do not know the outcome or end result, I know I will be SAFE—even if the result is my death.

God is taking me through a transformation, both inside and out.

He is continuously teaching me new things, and showing me the why in the form of revelations.

After I lost all that weight, none of my clothes fit, so I had to buy a completely new wardrobe. I look so different on the outside, and even more so now on the inside.

I have been trying to wear clothes that do not fit anymore... not by a long shot. I have never worn the clothes (spiritually), that He is laying out every day for me to wear, so I am uncomfortable and I squirm, and I try to be who I am not anymore. He showed me that I was still trying to be who I used to be (the nothing, the little boy), but I am now a Woman of God.

He showed me that I was still trying to be who I used to be (the nothing, the little boy), but I am now a Woman of God.

I needed to be shown that so I now can walk in who I am.

Walk in strength. Walk in confidence.

Head held high. Sword in hand.

The other revelation I got was that I have been trying to recognise Jesus as the majority see and recognise Him, as if that is better, (because the majority rules), but He said to me that if He wanted that for me, my life would be very different than it is and has been.

He reminded me that He has set me apart, and said that being set apart was different from being an outcast, although they may feel the same.

He reminded me that He has set me apart, and said that being set apart was different from being an outcast, although they may feel the same.

One is of God and the other is of man.

I love talking to Jesus. I love taking the time to be with Him. I love how He knows who I am before I even get there.

I love that I am never alone… never.

I did an online challenge to go deeper with Jesus. Through it, I got this message from Him,

You have been taught that I am angry, harsh, and impatient. You have been shamed, blamed, humiliated, and condemned.

All of the passion that I have for Jesus is directed towards you. Therefore, I declare that you also are My Beloved.

Beloved, you have found favour in My eyes because I only see the new you in Jesus. There is a place of delight in Me, where you may safely find rest in the understanding that I see you as a new person.

All the old has passed away, everything has become new, and this is My gift to you. The old you is dead. I give you permission to be dead to self, and to learn with Me, how to be alive only to Me!

Beloved, there is no struggle with the old you. He is gone.

Beloved, you have found favour in My eyes because I only see the new you in Jesus.

You are simply attached to a habit, a pattern of behaviour, memories and experiences from the world, the flesh, and the devil.

This cannot be broken by focusing on it. It remains through that focus. It can only be broken by the New Life that is already in you.

Just walk away from it. Focus on the new you.

Beloved, I will teach you to think in a way that re-

news your mind. The mind of Christ in you, is the best foundation for new beginnings.

My promises will cause you to thrive in life, regardless of the world around you. I have been raising up in you, an unstoppable hope. Hope fuels your fire of faith, and of love. Hope's breath is the very atmosphere of Heaven.

I have been raising up in you, an unstoppable hope. Hope fuels your fire of faith, and of love. Hope's breath is the very atmosphere of Heaven.

I see you through the eyes of First Love. This is your inner atmosphere. It is the environment We share with you. This is Our secret place with each other. We are delighted to draw you into the place of Our love and affection.

Nothing will ever separate you from Our love.

You complete My heart.

My whole life I have been searching for love, value, acceptance, purpose and safety. With the last four words of His message, He gave me everything I have ever yearned for.

You complete My heart.

It is unfathomable to comprehend that I could possibly complete His heart. How could little insignificant me, be that important to the God of all creation, the God of all things?

Yet, He says I am.

His words brought forth so much healing and they empowered me to keep going. As hard as it is, I choose to journey on to find the person who He sees when He looks at me. I choose to go deeper with Him. I choose to live out His purpose for my life. I choose Him.

His words brought forth so much healing and they empowered me to keep going. As hard as it is, I choose to journey on to find the person who He sees when He looks at me.

I know now that I am no longer a heart divided. I am no longer the person I used to be. As He said, I am a new creation, a new me.

Carmel. A Woman in God. A Woman of God.

Who He ordained and purposed me to be.

I am free to step out as the new me, knowing that when I stumble and fall on the trail of life, He will catch me, and help me back to my feet.

No condemnation. No fear. No shame.

Delight. Value. Trust. Strength. Courage. Truth.

At the start of this book, I was on the hunt for

victory. I thought victory would be defeating this sickness, but it has nothing to do with it at all. Instead of victory, I became a slave. A slave to the illness. A slave to the despair of it. I let it consume me. I gave in to it and it nearly destroyed me.

I think victory has less to do with me, and everything to do with Jesus.

He died for me. He redeemed me. He wears the Victor's crown.

So yeah, I have definitely found victory, because I have Him.

Through it all, He has given me the most amazing gifts.

Peace. Freedom. Courage. Wisdom. Truth. Grace.

I never again get to be alone. I get to live in safety without fear of the unknown.

I get to wear the title of Overcomer. Not because I beat the sickness, but because I overcame the hold it has on me. I do not fear what it can or may do to me. It holds no power over me anymore.

I get to wear the title of Overcomer. Not because I beat the sickness, but because I overcame the hold it has on me.

All that matters is my walk with Jesus.

Our relationship. Him and me.

I do not know how long my life's journey will be, nor where He may take me, but the one thing I do know is that I am definitely headed in the right direction.

I do not know how long my life's journey will be, nor where He may take me, but the one thing I do know is that I am definitely headed in the right direction.

I am,

Completely Accepted.

Completely Loved.

Completely Safe.

One day I will be a Heart Complete.

A Heart Complete in Jesus.

Every day, He still gives me the freedom to choose.

Because He is ever the gentleman and I am not a slave.

> *"The Spirit of the Sovereign Lord is on me, because the Lord has anointed me, to proclaim good news to the poor.*
>
> *He has sent me to bind up the broken-hearted, to proclaim freedom for the captives and release from darkness for the prisoners, to*

proclaim the year of the Lord's favour, and the day of vengeance of our God, to comfort all who mourn, and provide for those who grieve in Zion, ***to bestow on them a crown of beauty instead of ashes, the oil of gladness instead of mourning, and a garment of praise instead of a spirit of despair.*** *They will be called oaks of righteousness, a planting of the LORD for the display of His splendour."*

Isaiah 61:1-3

He has given me a crown of beauty to wear.
It is mine alone.
It bears the name He calls me.
"*My Beloved.*"